Original title:
Fruitful Gatherings

Copyright © 2025 Creative Arts Management OÜ
All rights reserved.

Author: Nolan Kingsley
ISBN HARDBACK: 978-1-80586-434-9
ISBN PAPERBACK: 978-1-80586-906-1

An Orchard's Legacy

In the orchard, apples laugh,
Their giggles sounding sweet,
Squirrels join the pie-shaped dance,
While bees buzz to the beat.

Grapes work hard to raise a toast,
While pears are drafting cheers,
Lemons squeeze out laughter loud,
As peaches pull some jeers.

Underneath the leafy shade,
Fruit flies play their pranks,
Throwing seeds at passing bees,
And doing fruitless janks.

When all the harvests done and gone,
Histories are spun,
The trees will tell their tales once more,
Of laughter, life, and fun.

Shared Plates of Time

Bananas slide across the table,
In a race that's oh so grand,
Meanwhile, oranges say "Don't peel!"
With a wink they take a stand.

Cherry tops are stacking high,
While berries scatter wide,
Pineapples juggle light and bright,
In this feast, they take pride.

Banquets filled with mushy jokes,
As pears begin to tease,
An apple tries a magic trick,
But falls down with a wheeze.

In a whirl of vibrant hues,
And laughter fills the air,
We gather close, share bites and smiles,
Creating joy to share.

Blushing Peaches

Peaches blush as they strut by,
With soft and fuzzy flair,
They giggle in their rosy dress,
No one can help but stare.

Plums roll around in laughter,
Holding court with great delight,
They juggle all their juicy jokes,
In the warm and sunny light.

Berries burst with tiny giggles,
Their courage full and bold,
They play the role of tiny clowns,
In a story to be told.

As summer fades and colors blend,
The fruits will not forget,
The jests and japes they shared in joy,
And memories, sweeter yet.

Echoes of the Orchard

In echoes of the orchard's song,
The fruits all hum along,
A jalopy cart rolls by in jest,
Pulling all the fruity throng.

Crisp apples tell of silly tales,
Of a stalker grape so sly,
While bananas peel back layers deep,
To share a tearful sigh.

Through winding paths of leafy cheer,
The laughter never wanes,
Oranges drop some teasing puns,
While apples hold their reins.

When dusk settles on the trees,
And shadows start to play,
The fruits will share one last good laugh,
Before they fade away.

Reflections in a Glass

Toast to the peas, they're quite the sight,
With tiny green jackets, they steal the night.
Carrots in costume, doing a jig,
Under the moon, they dance small and big.

Grapes are gossipers, hanging around,
Telling old tales without making a sound.
Oranges are rolling, oh what a chase,
Citrus and sweetness, a real wild race.

Tasting Life's Abundance

Strawberries giggle, they squish so near,
Fruit salad's a party, let's give a cheer!
Bananas play sax, what tunes they blow,
Cherries compete, putting on a show.

Lemons act sour, but don't take it hard,
They spice up the lemonade, that's their card.
Peaches are swaying, in laughter they thrive,
Sharing good vibes, they come alive.

Together in a Bounty

On picnic blankets, the feast is set,
Zucchini jokes, you won't soon forget.
Tomatoes are blushing, all ripe and red,
While corn on the cob plans what to spread.

Raspberries tease, with a tart little grin,
Whispering secrets, where to begin?
Watermelons belly flop, a splashy show,
In this fruity gathering, let friendship grow.

The Alliance of Nature

Nature's comedians, berries in line,
They pluck at our laughs like sunshine divine.
Kiwi's so fuzzy, a fuzzy old chap,
Wearing a smile, while grapes take a nap.

Avocados are scheming, in guacamole dreams,
Zesty and spicy, it's more than it seems.
With laughter and flavors, we join the fun,
Nature's great circus, the show just begun.

Savoring the Harvest

We laughed as we picked, oh what a thrill,
A basket of veggies, we'd soon spill.
Tomatoes like balls, ripe for the fight,
Our salad would surely reach a new height.

Carrots like swords, we paraded in cheer,
'A feast for the crows!' one shouted with sneer.
We tossed them in soup, then danced 'round the stew,
The kitchen a mess, but the flavors just flew.

Apple-Picking Adventures

In the orchard we climbed, with baskets in tow,
The apples were ripe, and our laughter did flow.
We slipped on some mud, oh what a sly fall,
Then rolled down the hill, bopping off walls.

The apples on trees seemed to laugh at our plight,
We picked some, then tasted, they sparkled in light.
With juice on our shirts and smiles galore,
We raced to the car, demanding for more!

The Aroma of Togetherness

With spices and fruits all around us there lay,
An aroma that beckoned, come join in the play.
We mixed up a cider, oh, what a blend!
Our skills in the kitchen would surely offend.

Laughter erupted as someone would slip,
The apples flew high, they soared like a ship.
With each chug of cider, our cheeks all did glow,
'Next time let's try it with pickles!' we crow.

Tasting Joy

In the kitchen we gathered, the table was set,
An assortment of goodies, the best feast yet.
We tasted each dish, with giggles and grins,
Who knew that avocado could lead to such sins?

The dessert was a pie that was far too large,
We tackled it bravely, like a fun-loving charge.
With crumbs on our faces and joy in our hearts,
We knew this was fun, where togetherness starts.

Harvesting Whispers

In the orchard where we play,
Giggles dance among the hay.
Pick a pear, take a chance,
Squirrels join in our fruit-filled dance.

Lemonade spills, oh what a sight,
Sun hats slipping, oh what a fright!
Bananas rolling down the hill,
Who's got the courage for the thrill?

Apples tumble, one by one,
Caught a pie crust, oh what fun!
Sticky fingers, laughter loud,
We're the fruit-looting, silly crowd.

When the sun begins to set,
All these memories, we won't forget.
Gather 'round with silly faces,
Where laughter sprouts in funny places.

Bounty's Embrace

In a field of cotton candy,
Jellybeans are oh-so-handy.
Tomatoes wear a silly frown,
As we twirl the veggies 'round.

Pumpkin hats, we take the prize,
Dancing in our big surprise.
Squash and carrots sing a tune,
While the corn jumps like a loon.

Chasing berries on the run,
Hoping for a raspberry bun.
Caught in laughter, what a scene,
With fruity friends, we're quite the team!

As the sun dips low, we cheer,
Sharing snacks, we hold so dear.
In this place where smiles expand,
We've harvested smiles, so unplanned!

Orchard Serenade

In the orchard, birds take flight,
Singing songs of sheer delight.
We mimic crows, with goofy glee,
Making pie jokes, just you and me.

Peaches giggle, grapes roll by,
Watermelon winks with a sly eye.
Cherries play a game of tag,
While the apples laugh and brag.

We swing from branches, oh, what fun,
Until a peach falls, then we run!
Laughter echoes, we lose our way,
In this silly, sunny play.

As twilight dances on the leaves,
With giggles stuck like honeybees.
We share our tales, oh so grand,
In this orchard, hand in hand.

The Sweetness of Unity

Gather 'round, it's party time,
With cupcakes and fruit that taste sublime.
Bananas slip, lemons giggle,
In this feast, our hearts just wiggle.

Lime-green hats and orange juice,
Slice the cake, and let it loose!
Strawberries sing a silly song,
In this gathering, we all belong.

Cinnamon rolls and pumpkin pies,
Sweetest laughter fills the skies.
Who knew joy could taste so sweet?
In this fun, we can't be beat!

As night falls, we toast and cheer,
For moments like this, we hold so dear.
In fruity laughter, united, we grow,
Our sweet memories, forever in tow.

A Symphony of Flavors

In the orchard, we pick our treats,
Lemonheads and cherry sweets.
Ripe tomatoes toss like balls,
Even weevils take the falls.

Bananas dance upon the ground,
Mangoes giggle, whoosh around.
Peaches throw their fuzz like darts,
While grapes play hopscotch on our carts.

A cabbage rolls, it starts to spin,
Juggling the fruit with a cheeky grin.
As apples plummet from trees high,
We dodge and duck, oh my, oh my!

In this dappled, wacky grove,
Every gatherer finds their trove.
With sticky hands and laughs so loud,
We share our bounty, feeling proud.

The Sweetness of Togetherness

Strawberries in a huddle laugh,
Slicing jokes like they're the half.
Pineapples wear their crowns so bold,
While melons hum their secrets told.

Cherries compete in a race so fast,
Twisting in circles, having a blast.
Lemons split into juicy quips,
Throwing zest like little skips.

Oranges roll with playful cheer,
Telling tales that all can hear.
As kumquats join with giggles bright,
We toast to friendship, what a sight!

In this banquet, the laughter flows,
Each sweet nibble, as love grows.
Under the sun, with all our joy,
We savor life, oh what a ploy!

Sheltered in Blossoms

In a treehouse made of berry dreams,
We sip on nectar, bursting seams.
Honeybees buzz with quirky tunes,
As lemons wear tiny hats and balloons.

Fruits all gathered, sharing tales,
Of windy days and funny fails.
Plums perform in a wobbly line,
While peaches tease, "A dance? Just fine!"

Petals float down like candy rain,
We giggle over sloshed champagne.
As grapefruits juggle seeds like stars,
We cheer for each, near and far.

Blossoms giggle and sway with glee,
In this hideaway, wild and free.
Under the shade, we paint our dreams,
In bursts of laughter and sunny beams.

A Tapestry of Seasons

Autumn brings its pumpkin pride,
While April grapes have skills to glide.
Straw hats tipped with fruits so ripe,
Funny faces, can't help but snipe.

Summer berries set the pace,
Wearing sunshine on their face.
Winter apples fan their tales,
In woolly hats and fuzzy veils.

Spring's ruckus with blooms galore,
Kiwis throwing tricks and more.
Everyone's gathered, friends unite,
Citrus quips make the fun ignite!

In this patchwork, bright and bold,
Laughter shared, stories told.
Through seasons' dance, we spin and sing,
Oh, what joy each gathering brings!

Unity in Abundance

In a field where apples roll,
We chase them with a silly goal.
One fell in my lemonade, oh dear!
Now it's a party drink, so cheer!

Peaches giggle as they drop,
On the heads that never stop.
Orange juice spills with a splash,
While the banana takes a dash.

Berries hide beneath the leaves,
Making mischief, what a tease!
Gathering laughter, making haste,
Who knew fruit could bring such taste?

All together, what a sight,
Every fruit a pure delight.
In this chaos, joy's the key,
Silly moments, oh so free!

Orchard Mysteries Unveiled

Why did the pear wear a hat?
Searching for the rumors 'that?
It's trying to look quite so grand,
The fashion trends of this fruit band.

Grapes formed a union, they declare,
With tiny suits, oh what a pair!
They roll around in a silly chase,
Telling jokes in a juicy space.

Bananas slip on their own peels,
While oranges share their best reels.
In this orchard, laughter reigns,
As every fruit dodges the rains.

Toward the sun, the fruits do prance,
Under the moon, they take a chance.
In the night, the fruits all cheer,
The orchard secrets, loud and clear!

The Art of Collecting

Bees buzz in and out of place,
While the lemons shine with grace.
Collecting laughter, tricks not small,
Whose turn is it to take the fall?

The plum's a joker, full of wit,
Making everyone laugh a bit.
While cherries giggle, round and red,
At the silly puns we've said!

Peach and apricot grab a seat,
At our table, feeling neat.
With tasty bites and joy to spare,
The sweetest moments fill the air.

Every fruit with a role to play,
At our gathering, come what may.
In this circus of colors bright,
We collect memories, pure delight!

Gathering Moments in the Grove

Under the trees, where shadows dance,
Grapes and figs steal a glance.
They plot a game of hide and seek,
With giggles that make the branches creak.

The plump avocados rave and shout,
As passion fruits spin all about.
Juggling seeds, they trip and fall,
What a show! Come one, come all!

Kiwi is singing a silly rhyme,
Attracting lots of fruit in time.
Gathered here with a laugh so loud,
The grove bursts forth with a cheering crowd.

As the sun sets, they take a bow,
Exhausted from fun, oh how!
In the grove where joy is spun,
Every gathering is pure fun!

Pomegranate Promises

In a garden full of laughter,
Pomegranates juggle in the breeze.
One dropped and splattered, oh what a mess!
Seeds everywhere, sweet as a tease.

We gather round with sticky hands,
Waging wars with juice that stains.
Who knew such fun was found in fruit?
Our laughter echoed, shaking our brains!

A fruit fight breaks, and oh what glee,
We throw the seeds with all our might.
The squirrels eye us in disbelief,
As we create our own delight.

With each burst, a giggle shared,
Pomegranate dreams, wild and free.
In this crazy garden of joyous pals,
We find our sweet serendipity.

Cedar and Citrus

In a grove where laughter lives,
Cedar shadows meet citrus calls.
Lemon peels fly like confetti,
While orange puns improvise our brawls.

We dance 'neath the branches, slipping feet,
Squeezed juice spritzed like laughter's rain.
Someone yells, 'I think I'm zest!'
We giggle, each squeeze causing a claim.

A grapefruit war starts, the roundest of all,
I duck and roll to catch my breath.
Witty barbs and citrus puns,
The kind of fun that feels like theft!

As we clean up the aftermath,
With sticky fingers and peels galore.
We'll remember this fruity laughter,
In the heart of woods we so adore.

Embers of Connection

Around the fire, we gather near,
With apples roasting, laughter in air.
A bite of warmth, a spark of cheer,
But one too hot, folks leave their chair!

"Hey, that apple's quite a star!"
Says Tim, who nearly faced the flames.
We all chuckle, a bit too loud,
Each round of jokes, igniting the games.

Banana peels become the score,
A slip, a fall, we all unite.
"Watch your step!" and giggles soar,
As fruity camaraderie ignites.

With marshmallows stuck to our clothes,
We share our tales under the moon.
Through sticky sweetness, bonds grow vast,
Our gathering turns to joyful tune.

The Richness of Nature's Platter

A basket full of nature's spoils,
We nibbled grapes and told tall tales.
With every bite, our laughter boiled,
As berries bounced from flimsy scales.

Peach juice dribbles down our chins,
"Oh dear, the dog just swiped a bite!"
We point and laugh, declare the win,
He's love-struck by our sweet delight.

Cherries pit-spit contest ensues,
Seeds flying high, creating mess.
Freckles pop on cheeks like jewels,
In this crazy, fruity fest!

So here we sit, with plates piled high,
With every chuckle, joy expands.
In nature's bounty, friendships tie,
Together always, life's sweet strands.

A Cornucopia of Laughter

In a basket teeming with glee,
Bananas giggle in jubilee.
Apples chuckle, red and round,
While oranges roll, not making a sound.

The grapes are glancing, what a sight,
Tickling each other, full of delight.
Pineapples wear a crown just for fun,
While cherries burst out, one by one.

Lemons squeeze in a playful punch,
As berries mimic every brunch.
A toast of laughter, what a spree,
Gathering joy, pure jubilee!

So let's dance with our fruity crew,
In a fiesta of flavors, that's nothing new!
With every bite, our giggles soar,
In this cornucopia, who could ask for more?

Celebrating Nature's Bounty

Underneath the sunny skies,
Tomatoes wiggle, what a surprise!
Carrots wear their leafy hats,
While celery plays with curious cats.

Pumpkins grin from their patchy land,
Creating chaos, isn't it grand?
Radishes joke, spicing the scene,
While peas giggle, oh so green!

A cabbage joins in, rolling down,
Chasing laughter all through the town.
As veggies gather, the fun won't stop,
Nature's bounty makes hearts hop!

So bring your forks and join the cheer,
In a garden party, all is clear!
With bites of joy, each taste a song,
Celebrating produce, all day long!

Threads of Sunlit Togetherness

In a patch of sunlit cheer,
Berries whisper, "Come right here!"
Strawberries dressed in red parade,
While blackberries laugh, a sweet charade.

Grapes are tangled in a spin,
Sipping juices, ready to begin.
Peaches primp with velvety flair,
While nectarines wink without a care.

A medley of colors, so bright to see,
Join the fun, come sip some tea!
Under the sun, laughter flows,
Threads together, as friendship grows.

So gather 'round for a fruity dance,
In this sun-kissed world, take a chance!
With every taste, smiles will weave,
In this patch of joy, we believe!

The Laughter of the Orchard

In the orchard, giggles sprout,
Where apples tease without a doubt.
Pears swing on branches high,
While plums joke as they pass by.

Cherries dance in a rosy line,
While apricots giggle, feeling fine.
The nuts crack up, it's quite the show,
As peach trees sway to and fro.

Oranges play hopscotch in the sun,
While dandelions join in the fun.
Each laughter carries on the breeze,
Tickling the souls of the trees.

So come join the merry crew,
In this orchard, joy shines through!
With every joke, we share our hearts,
A laughter-filled day, where joy starts!

Harvesting Memories

In the orchard, laughter grows,
We pick the fruit, not our toes.
A juicy splash, what a scene,
Who knew pears could be so mean?

Mangoes rolling, off the truck,
Is it bad luck or just bad luck?
Bananas slip while we all cheer,
Now we're dancing, never fear!

Baskets overflowing with delight,
Jams and jellies taking flight.
Grandma's recipe – oh what a treat,
Ketchup's a fruit? What a feat!

Underneath this fruity sun,
We gather round for some good fun.
With every bite, a story told,
Harvested memories, worth more than gold.

The Gathered Scents of Nature

In the garden, scents collide,
Tomatoes burst – oh what a ride!
Cucumbers giggle, peas all shout,
Did you hear that? Something's sprouting out!

Dill and thyme, they have a chat,
Mr. Carrot tips his hat.
Basil sneezes, what a sight,
Lavender waves with all its might!

A picnic blanket, crumbs all here,
Sticky fingers, joyful cheer.
Ants and bees join in the fun,
A fruit fight, who's the last one?

So grab a pie, or even a cake,
Nature's scents, what a break!
Friends and laughter, side by side,
Together we'll take this silly ride.

Merlot Moonlight

Under stars, a gathering rare,
We sip on dreams, with a flair.
Red wine spills, oh what a blast,
Is that a grape or did you cast?

Cheese and crackers, they make a mess,
While someone's trying to impress.
A cork pops loud, we all will cheer,
Hoping nobody spills their beer!

Chasing shadows, full of jest,
Merlot moonlight - can't resist the fest.
With giggles floating through the air,
Who knew we were such a perfect pair?

Laughter echoes, glasses clink,
Inhibitions gone - we just think!
The night grows old, but laughter stays,
With every sip, a silly phase.

The Savoring of Togetherness

Around the table, laughter's spread,
As mashed potatoes fly like lead.
Gravy rivers, kinfolk dive,
Who's the fastest? Who's alive?

Corn on the cob, we race to bite,
It's a veggie war, what a sight!
Pass the peas, then take a scoop,
Watch out! Here comes the fruit loop!

Tarts and pies, oh what a feat,
The cherry one's a tasty treat.
But who forgot to buy the ice?
Now it's melting—what a price!

Yet through the chaos, we all find,
A love that's joyful and so blind.
In this mess, we truly see,
Together's where we long to be.

Nectar of Kinship

Cousins crunch on apples bright,
Squeezing juice, oh what a sight!
Auntie's pie is just too sweet,
While Uncle's dance has two left feet.

Siblings share a bowl of grapes,
With silly hats, making shapes.
Laughter flies as snacks collide,
We save the last slice, who could decide?

Giggling while the blender whirs,
As smoothies swirl in vibrant blurs.
We sip and spill, oh what a mess,
Who knew family could be such a guess?

In the kitchen, chaos reigns,
With jelly stains on our remains.
But all this joy, a sweet embrace,
In every bite, our love's in place.

A Mosaic of Edible Dreams

Juicy berries on a tray,
Squabbles break out, who'll have the say?
Mango slices, bright and round,
Whispers of laughter all around.

Gran's pecan pie, a famous hit,
Yet cousin Joe thinks he can outwit.
With whipped cream fights, we aim for fun,
Who knew this gathering would weigh a ton?

Chips and dip are flying fast,
Each giant spoonful, a true blast.
Uncle's jokes are truly absurd,
As auntie's fruit salad shakes the herd.

Through spilled drinks and playful shouts,
We savor love that never doubts.
Our plates piled high, a grand delight,
Edible love makes everything right.

Harvesting Whispers

Gather 'round, it's time to cheer,
For juicy watermelon here!
Cousin Pete thinks he'll impress,
But trips on fruit—oh what a mess!

Peach cobbler brothers love to bake,
Yet spelling flour's a big mistake.
Mom laughs as flour clouds the air,
We're all a bit sticky, but who would care?

Grapes are tossed like little balls,
Who catches them? We make those calls.
Sister yells, "I'm a grape queen!"
As giggles dance, like never seen.

In these moments, laughter flows,
In every bite, our love just grows.
With crumbs and joy, we gather near,
Harvesting whispers, oh so dear.

Baskets of Dreams

In baskets full of colors bright,
We gather under the sun's warm light.
Pineapples land as chairs clog the lane,
Uncle's dance moves create a chain.

Cherries bouncing, watch them roll,
Siblings race to grab the whole bowl.
Fruit stands tall like a funny game,
With berry fights and laughter the same.

Jokes are sliced like lemon zest,
Auntie's punch? You'll never guess.
Refills needed, but who's to say,
These gigs can last all day!

With every fruit and every grin,
As family gathers, the fun begins.
Through fruity chaos, we find our dreams,
In every giggle, laughter beams.

Colors of Community

In a garden full of cheer,
Neighbors gather, never fear.
Tomatoes roll, and laughter flies,
As bell peppers play dress-up in the skies.

Zucchinis dance a silly jig,
While radishes wear hats so big.
Squash jokes sprout between the rows,
And eggplants pose in stylish clothes.

Onions cry, but never pout,
Broccoli's here, no need to doubt.
The carrots cheer in colors bright,
A parade of veggies, pure delight!

Everyone's munching, what a feast,
With a side of laughter, not the least.
Gather 'round, it's time to play,
These veggies know how to slay the day!

An Infusion of Hues

Berries bounce in bowls so round,
Cherries giggle, what a sound!
Peaches blush, they're feeling sweet,
While lemons roll their pucker feat!

In the mix, a splash of fun,
Grapes are racing, on the run.
Melons slice in laughter's spree,
Tropical fruits join in with glee.

Smoothies whirl in colors bright,
Each sip's a new delight!
Pineapples wear their crowns with pride,
As laughter flows, we toss aside.

Gathering round to toast the taste,
This fruity crew, we won't waste.
With a giggle and a cheer,
Let's celebrate, our joy is here!

Petals and Palates

Daisies frolic in the grass,
While daisies tease the hesitant sass.
Nasturtiums spice up the show,
Their petals wink, 'Come join the flow!'

The herbs join in a fragrant dance,
Basil twirls, it's worth the chance.
Chive with flair, a green mustache,
While thyme takes selfies, oh what a clash!

In this garden, it's all a game,
With lavender bringing a pop of fame.
Rosemary's poetry fills the air,
And marigolds smile without a care.

A potluck blooms with every hue,
As veggies stir a funny brew.
With petals bright and giggles strong,
In this gathering, we all belong!

The Blessing of Nature's Pluck

Nature's treasures, fresh and bright,
Tangled fun, what a sight!
Fruits and laughter, side by side,
In this chaos, we take pride.

Apples tumble, oranges roll,
Bouncing pears are in control.
A grapevine swings, oh what a ride,
While fig leaves hide in giggly stride.

Bananas peel and slip away,
Lemons squirt, or so they say.
Gatherings full of juicy tales,
In this colorful land, joy prevails!

So let us toast with fruity cheer,
To all the fun we hold so dear.
From every branch, let laughter pluck,
In nature's bounty, we find our luck!

Symphony of Taste and Togetherness

In the kitchen, we assemble, what a sight,
With chop and dice, it feels so right.
Avocados gossip, bananas joke,
Tomatoes chuckle, oh what a stroke!

Lemon drops a beat, it's getting loud,
Kiwi joins in, feeling proud.
A mix of flavors, a wild parade,
Never thought cooking was such a charade!

Garlic's funky dance, can't be ignored,
Herbs talking nonsense, oh, how they adored.
A symphony of taste, a joyous fuss,
With every bite, we can't help but discuss!

Laughter and spices twirl in the air,
In this crazy kitchen, we have not a care.
As we feast together, the flavors collide,
In our happy gathering, we take it in stride!

Gathering at Day's End

As the sun sets down and the stars take flight,
Friends round the table, oh what a sight!
Chips in one bowl, salsa in another,
We share our stories like no one can smother.

A giant fruit salad, a colorful heap,
With watermelon jokes that cut rather deep.
Pineapple wears sunglasses, what a fun guise,
While pears in a corner start telling tall lies!

Everyone's nibbling, a giggle or two,
As apples proclaim, they're the best in the crew.
They argue and squabble, this bickering fair,
While strawberries giggle, with juice in the air!

Dusk wraps us in laughter, with a sweet gentle sway,
With every sweet morsel, the worries decay.
Our gathering of flavors, a banquet of cheer,
At day's end we munch, with friends we hold dear!

The Aroma of Shared Fruits

Once upon a market, ripe fruits did sway,
Mingling aromas in a zesty ballet.
Honeydew whispers, "Come take a whiff!"
While oranges juggle, and laugh with a tiff!

Cherries pop in, 'It's sweet-tastic fun!'
Grabbing the spotlight, they dance in the sun.
Lemons roll around, plotting a scheme,
To sour the others, or so it would seem!

Banana cracks jokes, the peel on his face,
"Without us, dear friends, what would be your taste?"
Pineapples nod, knowing they hold the crown,
Together they laugh, never wearing a frown!

In this fragrant fiesta, we munch and we chat,
As the bonds of our laughter grow thicker than fat.
The aroma of joy, of laughter and cheer,
Reminds us that sharing is what we hold dear!

Embracing Nature's Riches

In the orchard we gather, with laughter and glee,
Picking juicy treasures, as happy as can be.
Apples and peaches, in baskets they lie,
While berries are ready to give pie a try!

Nature serves up a colorful feast,
With grapes in the mix, we're never the least.
Sneaky rabbits watch, from behind the tree,
While we munch on our snacks, carefree and free!

"Who dropped that one?" an orange did yell,
With a zest for life, it's quite the tale to tell.
As we share our bounty, partaking the fun,
With smiles all around, our laughter weighs a ton!

In the embrace of nature, the day drifts away,
Amidst giggles and crunches, we're here to stay.
These simple moments, stitched with such grace,
With a wink and a bite, we've found our place!

Echoing Laughter in the Orchard

In the orchard's bright embrace,
Apples giggle, what a chase!
Pears and plums play hide and seek,
Chasing squirrels, oh so cheek!

Bouncing berries crack a joke,
While oranges dance, the laughter woke.
Grapes on vines, in clusters tight,
Whisper secrets, oh what a sight!

Peaches blush, with cheeky flair,
While lemons pucker, unaware.
Cherries chuckle, swinging free,
In this orchard, joy's decree!

Melons roll with silly grace,
As laughter echoes in this place.
Lemons giggle, grappling woes,
In this harvest, laughter grows!

The Festivals of Flavors

Banana hats and kiwi shoes,
At the fair, there's no excuse!
Pineapple crowns parade in style,
While all fruits dance with a smile!

Citrus spritzers spark delight,
Lime and ginger, what a sight!
Tomatoes juggle, red as fire,
With each toss, they never tire!

Strawberries serenade the crowd,
While blueberries sing, bold and loud.
Raspberry pies spin round and round,
In this festival, joy is found!

Fruit punch splashes, colors bright,
As everyone's face shines with light.
With a wink, the mangoes cheer,
Together, we spread the fun here!

An Assembly of Seasons

In spring's light, the berries bloom,
With laughter filling every room!
Cherries giggle, dressed in red,
While the bees dance overhead!

Summer's heat, a citrus fair,
Lemons prance without a care.
Peaches pop with giggly glee,
Watermelons rolling free!

Autumn calls with crunchy leaves,
Pumpkins chuckle, oh how they tease!
Apples bobbing in the breeze,
Gathering joy with such ease!

Winter's chill brings citrus cheer,
Oranges smiling, "We are here!"
In every season, laughter rings,
An assembly where joy springs!

Cornucopia of Memories

A basket brimming with delight,
Bananas winking, oh, what a sight!
Mangoes sharing tales of sun,
In this bounty, laughter's spun!

Grapefruits chat over morning brew,
Subtle jokes in every hue.
Peppers dance, a zesty thrill,
While pickles make us laugh until!

As carrots tell their leafy tales,
Radishes giggle; joy prevails.
Corn pops in a merry tale,
Each crunch brings laughter, without fail!

A feast of memories, carved in cheer,
With every bite, the fun draws near.
In this cornucopia, we convene,
Celebrating all that's bright and green!

Trees as Witnesses

Trees stand tall, they saw it all,
From squirrels' dance to the pie tree fall.
Laughing leaves in the autumn breeze,
Whispering secrets with such great ease.

A cat snuck in, stole the picnic spread,
While birds chirped loud, full of mischief ahead.
Beneath their boughs, the laughter would flare,
The trees just chuckled, branches in the air.

With every bite, another tale spun,
As ants formed lines, joining in on the fun.
The sunlight glowed, not a care in sight,
Nature's own comedy, pure delight.

So let us gather, let the stories ring,
The trees will listen, and perhaps they'll sing.
For every mishap, each humorous scene,
Will echo through leaves, a joyous routine.

Gathering Under Fig Branches

Beneath the figs, where shadows play,
We chew on gossip and fruit every day.
A fruit fly buzzed, stole a bite with glee,
"Hey! That was mine!" yelled a laugh from me.

But figs are generous, they laugh right back,
As juice drips down on a picnic snack.
Splatters and giggles beneath the green,
The silliest scene you've ever seen!

One branch gave in, we fell in a heap,
Among the laughter, not a soul would weep.
A puppy dashed in, grabbed our last tart,
With all of this joy, who needs a sweet heart?

So here we sit, under branches so wide,
With nature laughing, nothing left to hide.
In this fruity chaos, we'll sing and we'll shout,
Gathering joy is what it's all about.

Juicy Reflections

In the mirror of juice, we see ourselves,
A melon face, with berry-stained shelves.
"Who looks best?" we joke, with sticky hands,
As each tries to pose, pulling funny strands.

Grapes roll away, causing a balloon,
A tumble of laughter, beneath the full moon.
Citrus laughs bright, all zesty and bold,
While banana slips in, adding warmth to the cold.

Paper straws bend, a bendy brigade,
While cherries chuckle, not shy to parade.
A fruit salad chorus, a symphony strange,
In every sweet jar, hilarious change.

So pour another cup, let the jokes unfold,
With juicy reflections, we're never too old.
Let laughter bubble, let happiness pour,
In this fruity carnival, there's always more!

Wine and Whispers

With glasses clinked and laughter loud,
We sip our dreams beneath the crowd.
The cork pops off with a cheerful cheer,
As wine flows freely, erasing all fear.

Whispers abound of tales long gone,
Of slippery slopes and singing dawns.
One friend swears the grape told a lie,
"Blame the wine!" we all cry with a sigh.

A drop on the shirt, a giggle or two,
"Is it fashion?" she asks, as we squeal "No way, dude!"
Beneath twinkling stars, the night gets alive,
In vino veritas, we laugh and we thrive.

So let's raise a glass to the laughter we find,
With wine and sweet whispers, all intertwined.
In this merry chaos, we dance and we sing,
With every sip shared, a new joy takes wing.

Kisses of the Sky

The clouds are fluff, just like our dreams,
Bouncing around like silly beams.
With every giggle, the sun peeks out,
What's that? A kite? Oh, what a clout!

We gather here, a merry crew,
Chasing rainbows—yes, we do!
We trip on air, we dance and sway,
Laughing, singing, through the day!

The breeze carries jokes from far and wide,
With every gust, there's more to abide.
We munch on clouds, oh what a feast,
Silliness reigns; to joy, we're leased!

As the sun dips low, the stars ignite,
Our laughter echoes through the night.
In our little world, we're all so spry,
With kisses of the sky, we soar up high!

Under the Arbor of Friendship

Oh, what fun beneath this tree,
Where friends come together, wild and free.
We share our snacks in goofy bites,
While telling tales of silly heights.

The branches pose like our old pals,
They sway while we make all the howls.
We tease the squirrels, with acorns, too,
They scurry away, our antics flew!

Under the shade, the mischief grows,
From secret laughs to toe-pinching woes.
Here every smile's a little prank,
In this happy place, we love to rank!

As dusk falls softly, our voices blend,
In this dear space, we won't pretend.
Together we bloom, like flowers divine,
Under this arbor, forever we shine!

The Roundtable of Harvest

Around the table, we gather 'round,
With baskets of laughter, our joy is found.
Corn on the cob and pies so sweet,
With every bite, we dance on our feet!

The gourds tell tales of silly squabbles,
As we munch on crunchies, our laughter bobbles.
"Who stole the peas?" yells a voice so bright,
Like squirrels, we pounce in our playful plight!

Tomatoes roll in a little race,
Down the table, oh, what a chase!
With fun, we feast, and the cider flows,
Each toast a whiff of our silly prose.

As twilight blankets our cheeky feast,
We toast to the joy that never ceased.
At this roundtable, we're bond and cheer,
Harvesting laughter year after year!

Lemon Zest Adventures

Zest so bright, it tickles the nose,
Lemonade laughter just overflows.
With straws like swords, we wage our play,
In a citrus world, we dance and sway!

We slip on peels like banana clowns,
Tumbling around in our funny gowns.
"Who's next?" we shout, on this zesty quest,
With giggles and winks, we're all so blessed!

From lemon fields to pie-filled skies,
Each tart of joy makes our spirits rise.
We squeeze the day, make sour a thrill,
Balancing sweetness with our wild will.

So gather 'round for this zesty spree,
With juicy giggles, we're wild and free!
In the land of lemons, fun is the aim,
Adventurous hearts, forever the same!

The Orchard's Embrace

In the orchard's merry maze,
Squirrels dance in sunlit rays,
They gather snacks and make a fuss,
While birds gossip without a trust.

With apples plump and peaches round,
The laughter echoes, joy is found,
But watch your head, a pear might fall,
Watch out, or you'll be in their brawl!

Lemons squirt with cheerful glee,
As tiny ants hold a grand tea spree,
The plums roll down like sneaky thieves,
While everyone doubts their leafy sheaves.

Amidst the chaos, friendships bloom,
In every corner, laughter zooms,
The harvest yields a playful sport,
In every bite, the fun consorts.

Juicy Futures

Future plans in fruity dreams,
Bananas plot with silly schemes,
The oranges juice up their acts,
While grapefruits hold their juicy pacts.

In the distance, a melon sighs,
Wishing for sunny, slice-filled skies,
But cherries giggle, round and bright,
As they dress up for the night!

A pineapple's crown, regal and proud,
Looks down at the antics of the crowd,
As kiwis sneak in with fuzzy feet,
And they all join for a fun, wild treat.

Sliced visions of fruity delight,
In every scoop, a merry bite,
The future's bright, or so they say,
With fruity laughter leading the way.

Serendipity in the Grove

In the grove, where giggles grow,
Berries tumble with a showy glow,
Each vine holds secrets of sweet surprise,
As butterflies flirt and dragonflies rise.

Pinecones gossip, what's the news?
While peaches mingle with juicy views,
A mishap here, a funny blunder,
As fruit flies scatter, loud as thunder!

Orchard antics lead to zest,
Where every pear thinks it's the best,
The pruning shears they all outsmart,
In a game of hide-and-seek, they start.

Unexpected twirls and fruity pranks,
Nature's laughter fills the banks,
Serendipity reigns, the sun shines bright,
In a grove where joy takes flight!

Plucking Time's Bounty

Plucking treasures from the trees,
Everyone laughs, a joyful tease,
With baskets swinging, laughter flows,
While nature plays its silly shows.

The apples roll, no one's fazed,
Orange peels create a maze,
"Catch me if you can!" they shout,
While juicy chaos kicks about!

Bouncing peaches in a race,
A giggling worm finds its place,
With all this fun, who needs a feast?
Just grab a branch and join the beast!

Beneath the sun, our laughter rings,
In every nook where joy still clings,
We gather all, with hearts so light,
Plucking memories, pure delight!

The Joy of Picking Together

Under the tree, we laugh and play,
Bouncing around like apples in May.
Chasing the squirrels, they chatter and flee,
Who knew this fruit hunt would be so carefree?

Buckets in hand, we gather and grin,
One more pie, let the baking begin!
But wait, what's that? A berry on your nose,
You look like a clumsy berry-bush prose!

Friends turn to partners; the orchard's our stage,
We pick and we toss, just like a rampage.
Did you see that? A peach fell with flair,
We laugh till we cry, what a silly affair!

As dusk starts to fall, and the shadows grow long,
We dance through the grove, singing our song.
With buckets now full, we toast to good measure,
To the joy of this harvest, oh what a treasure!

Harvest Moon's Invitation

The moon grins wide, casting light on the field,
With buckets we frolic, our teamwork revealed.
Like corn on the cob, we pop with delight,
Picking under the stars, everything feels right.

Each fruit that we pluck brings giggles and cheer,
But watch out for the bees that seem to draw near!
They buzz like they own the place, what a show,
I'd rather be one with the apples, I know!

A cider toast shared with friends all around,
These gatherings bright, such joy can be found.
But careful with the punch, don't spill it, my mate,
Or we'll dance in the orchard until it gets late!

The harvest moon smiles, its job is quite clear,
To bring us together with laughter and cheer.
So shake off that basket; let's play in the hay,
And pack all our worries and troubles away!

Picking Memories

Remember that time we got lost in the grove?
We laughed 'til we cried, feeling just like a trove.
With apples in hand, we tumbled in hay,
Creating sweet memories, come join our ballet!

There's juice on your cheek; now when did that land?
A sticky reminder of this fruitful band.
We gather the goodies, our laughter the proof,
Make way for the dance; we're the orchard's goof!

Fresh lemonade spills; oh, what a mistake!
The bees strike up a dance for our folly to bake.
But hey, even spills can bring joy, it seems,
With laughter and giggles, we're living our dreams!

So here's to our trips through the fields and the trees,
To friends and to fun, with laughter the breeze.
Let's fill up our baskets, our hearts, and our days,
With memories sweet as a warm summer haze!

Uniting the Season's Gifts

Here comes October, the harvest parade,
With pumpkins and laughter, we're all quite amazed!
Silly scarecrows grin as we wander about,
Unite with the season, there's fun all about!

A tug on my sleeve, it's a friend in disguise,
With a pie on their head, oh what a surprise!
We gather and giggle, and soon we will bake,
A feast from the orchard is ours for the take!

As friends in the orchard, we twirl and we spin,
With baskets of goodies, our laughter won't thin.
The fruit may be ripe, but it's joy that we seek,
In this melting pot of flavors, we speak!

So come share this bounty, both humble and grand,
With laughter like apples, oh isn't it grand?
In every sweet moment, our hearts take the stage,
This gathering's a treasure that age cannot wage!

The Symphony of Ripening Days

In the orchard, laughter rings,
As apples tell of silly things.
Pears dance like they're on a spree,
While cherries giggle in the tree.

Beneath the sun, the berries scheme,
Wishing they'd invented cream.
Peaches toss their fuzzy hair,
While plums pretend to not care.

Grapes gather for a wild race,
Hopping quick with ample grace.
They all join in a joyful cheer,
As ripe delights draw everyone near.

And at the end of all the fun,
They'll toast with juice and shout, "Well done!"
In this patch, we all shall play,
In the symphony of ripening day.

Relishing Sun-drenched Now

Sticky fingers, sweet delight,
Juicy bites from morning light.
Lemons chuckle, tart and bold,
While watermelon jokes unfold.

Pineapples wear their crowns so high,
With coconut dreams that flutter by.
Bananas slip and laugh so loud,
As kids gather in a cheerful crowd.

Mangoes join the summer dance,
Wiggling as they take a chance.
Kiwis whisper secret tales,
As laughter rides the wind like sails.

Oh, what joy the harvest brings,
In sunny spots, we dance like kings!
With every bite, we shout hooray,
Relishing this sun-drenched day!

Gatherings in the Glade

In the glade, the laughter flows,
As fruits engage in silly shows.
Ripe to burst with juicy pride,
Imagine all the fun inside!

Berries dress in colors bright,
Strawberries ready for a fight.
Blueberries bubble up with glee,
While raspberries tease the bumblebee.

Oranges roll with vibrant zest,
Competing who can bounce the best.
Peach and apricot join the fray,
While chaos reigns in sunny play.

The sun peeks through the leafy veil,
As fruits all share a wild tale.
In the glade, together we stay,
In gatherings that make our day!

Nature's Shared Harvest

Under trees, a jolly crew,
Tomatoes roll, a comical view.
Pumpkins laugh with big, round glee,
As garlic shares its wild decree.

Carrots dig deep, out of sight,
Playful roots bring pure delight.
Onions join, and one turns red,
While radishes nod their plump heads.

Squash slips in with a grand shout,
While beans get tangled, sprouting clout.
In nature's harvest, joy ignites,
With friendships blooming, hearts take flight.

So let's celebrate these moments clear,
With veggies laughing, full of cheer.
In this shared embrace, we thrive,
Nature's harvest keeps us alive!

Picking Moments

In a field of giggling glee,
We pluck some joy from the tree.
Each laugh a berry, sweet and round,
With silly faces all around.

The grass tickles as we bend low,
A dance of fumbles, to and fro.
With every snip, a chuckle shared,
This jolly harvest is well prepared.

Baskets full, we start to boast,
Of funny slips, we laugh the most.
But when the weight is far too much,
We tumble down—oh, such a crutch!

Now meandering home, a merry crowd,
With stories swirling, lively and loud.
The moments picked, we hold so dear,
A feast of humor, year by year.

Nature's Tapestry of Hearts

In the garden where giggles bloom,
We weave our tales, dispelling gloom.
With butterflies as our silly crew,
We craft a quilt of laughter, too.

Tomatoes blush like late-night pranks,
While we hide behind the leafy ranks.
"Catch me if you can!" one shouts with glee,
As we dash beneath the cherry tree.

A beetle spins a dance so bright,
We mimic it, and oh, what a sight!
Nature giggles in a sunny spree,
A patchwork of joy, just you and me.

As day fades into twilight's grace,
We gather round and share our space.
With hearts aglow and tales that start,
Life's vibrant weave, a work of art.

Vibrant Tides of Togetherness

Under the sun, we splash and play,
Building castles in a silly way.
With giggles rolling like ocean waves,
In this tide of fun, we all are braves.

The buckets hold our evening dreams,
And laughter spills like sunny streams.
We dive for treasures, what a blast!
Collecting memories, oh, what a cast!

The seabreeze whirls, a joker's laugh,
As seagulls join our silly staff.
With sandy toes and salty hair,
Each moment cherished, everywhere.

As sunset paints the sky with cheer,
We gather close, our friends so near.
In vibrant tides, our bonds grow strong,
Each laugh a note in nature's song.

Savoring Autumn's Palette

Leaves like confetti, swirling down,
We stomp and twirl in our leaf crown.
Pumpkins giggle with silly grins,
As we feast on tangy apple skins.

Cider spills in splashes bright,
A prank gone wrong? Oh, what a sight!
With every sip, a laugh erupts,
As we dance with glee, no way to stop!

The bonfire crackles with spirited tales,
As marshmallow battles become our gales.
In this cozy nook, we share our heart,
Ah, savoring moments, oh, a fine art!

As night wraps us in its soft embrace,
We tuck in warmth, a laughter race.
In autumn's glow, we grasp and hold,
These vibrant memories, pure as gold.

The Fellowship of Ripe Fruit

In a bowl they all collide,
Bananas, cherries side by side.
Grapes chatter in a sweet debate,
While apples laugh and roll on straight.

All the berries start to dance,
Mango spins, it takes a chance.
Lemon rolls its eyes in glee,
As pear does its best to flee.

Pineapple wears a prickly crown,
Declaring this the juiciest town.
Everyone's a little nutty,
With laughter bright and oh so gutty.

But when the sorbet comes around,
All the fruit fall to the ground.
They slip and slide with gleeful shrieks,
Chasing sweetness for a week!

Sweet Serenades Beneath the Leaves

Underneath the trees we sway,
Plucking fruits in a silly play.
Giggling as we climb and dive,
Each bite makes the taste buds thrive.

Coconut tries to crack a joke,
While figs are busy getting woke.
An orange sings a citrus tune,
And all the apples join the swoon.

Cherry drapes in a rosy pout,
As everyone begins to shout.
Watermelon claims the throne,
Winking from his juicy zone.

Beneath friendship's leafy dome,
Each fruit finds its way back home.
Sweetness lingers in the air,
As laughter wraps us in its care.

Mulberry Dreams

In a patch of purple delight,
Mulberries dream under starlight.
They whisper tales to one another,
Of sweet love and juicy blunder.

Raspberry's a cheeky tease,
While blackberry flits through the trees.
Strawberry sneaks a sip of dew,
And giggles at the daily brew.

Boasting tales of sweetest vines,
They share the gossip with the pines.
Each berry shines in nature's play,
Turning ordinary into yay!

But when morning starts to rise,
Mulberries hug with sleepy sighs.
They dream of pies and syrupy streams,
Riding high on berry dreams.

Unity in Every Bite

Gather all your favorite picks,
Banana splits and fruity tricks.
In the bowl, flavors collide,
With each bite, a joyful ride.

Peach and nectarine gossip away,
While kiwi's always here to play.
Grapefruit's bittersweet surprise,
Makes everyone grin and close their eyes.

Avocado jumps in for some zest,
Declaring that it's simply the best.
Together they form a medley grand,
Taking us all to Flavor Land.

As bowls empty and laughter swells,
Each bite casts a magical spell.
In every juicy piece we share,
Is a bond that fills the air.

Collective Abundance

In a bowl of laughter, we toss and we mix,
Each bite a giggle, a plate full of tricks.
Bananas wear hats, cherries dance in delight,
A nutty brigade, ready to party all night.

Lemonade showers, we sip and we snort,
Citrus confetti thrown in every report.
We're the fruit squad with a jolly good plan,
Juicy shenanigans, come join while you can!

Mangoes play tag under the sun's bright cheer,
Potato chip crickets sing loud from the rear.
With grapes in our pockets, we're ready to roam,
At this gathering place, we always feel home.

So let's fill our baskets with mirth and big laughs,
A buffet of joy, let's write down our paths.
With our smoothies afloat, we toast to our crew,
And bite into life, fruity fun just for you!

The Orchard of Connections

Sipping sweet cider beneath a tall tree,
Where giggles and fruit flies are wild and carefree.
Pickles with grapefruits? Oh what a sight!
We dance like a salad, all dressed up for night.

The apples are gossiping, juicy and loud,
While plums tell the oranges, 'We're feeling quite proud!'
Berries in berets, putting on a show,
With winks from the cosmos, they steal the whole flow.

Olive oil winks at the fresh garlic clove,
And carrots in shades cheer as they groove.
Lemon zest plays on a zesty kazoo,
In this orchard of nonsense, there's fun just for you!

So gather your pals, the more, the merrier,
In this chuckle-filled heap, our hearts grow superior.
With fruit-themed jokes, let's sauce up the laugh,
In this orchard of smiles, let's craft our own path!

Tapestry of Flavors

With colors like rainbows, we spin and we tease,
A tapestry woven with giggles and cheese.
Pineapples in pajamas, what a sight to behold,
Waving to toasters, 'We're dazzling and bold!'

Strawberries plotting a silky escape,
While kiwi wigs jiggle, a fruity landscape.
Cherries pair with cupcakes, sweet talents outshine,
Together we giggle, our flavors combine.

Yogurt and honey are crafting a scene,
As cupcakes in frolics twirl quaintly and keen.
This patchwork of taste is slathered with cheer,
Each nibble a joy, let's all grab a beer!

We bounce into bliss, wearing laughter like crowns,
In this garden of flavors, nobody frowns.
So scoop up your pals for a musical moan,
In this tapestry vibrant, you'll never be alone!

Unity Beneath the Fruit-Laden Branches

Underneath the branches, we gather in style,
With punchlines and snacks that go on for a mile.
The grapes on the vine play hide and seek well,
And apples tell stories that ring like a bell.

Bananas are slipping on jokes that we share,
Peaches join in with a soft, silly flair.
Kiwi and coconut plotting a caper,
With giggles aplenty, they spin tales with paper.

The pie crust is smiling, flitting about,
As custard clouds drift with a giggly shout.
We're all fruit friends in this tree of delight,
With laughter as ripe as the stars in the night.

So rally your comrades, let joy be our guide,
With each slice of happiness, let spirit abide.
Beneath these great branches, let's cheer, make it loud,
In unity's orchard, let's gather the crowd!

Grapes Beneath the Sun

In a vineyard, we danced with glee,
Sipping juice, as wild as can be.
A bunch of grapes swayed in the breeze,
Their secrets whispered like rustling leaves.

We dared each other for a grape feast,
With sticky fingers, we laughed the least.
Slipping and sliding, our wine glasses spill,
Who knew fruit could give such a thrill?

Under the sun, the laughter grew,
With fermented giggles, we formed a crew.
The vines nodded in our merry chat,
As someone tripped over the nearby cat.

In the end, we toasts with the greenest of cheer,
To moments like this, we hold so dear.
A grape celebration, what a sight,
With laughter that danced into the night.

Bonding Over Blossoms

In a garden of blooms, we gathered with flair,
Sniffing the flowers, in laughter, we share.
A bee buzzed by with a curious sting,
Claiming a petal, like it owned the spring.

Amid blossoms bright, jokes flew like kites,
We painted the air with floral delights.
Who knew the daisies could gossip so loud,
About garden critters and laughter avowed?

A sunflower winked, oh what a tease,
Claiming best friend to the wayward breeze.
We swayed with the tulips, a wacky dance,
In a floral fiesta, we took our chance.

So here's to the blooms, both silly and sweet,
Each petal a giggle, a fragrant retreat.
In the heart of the garden, friendships bloom,
With laughter and petals, we brighten the room.

The Nectar of Kindred Spirits

Beneath the boughs, where the honey hangs,
We laughed and stumbled in our silly gangs.
With sticky fingers and faces aglow,
We joked about bees in a fruity show.

A spoonful of nectar turned sticky and bright,
We spread it on bread, what a comical sight!
Spilling the honey with each loving jest,
The kindred spirits put taste to the test.

With every dip and a giggle exchanged,
Our bond grew stronger, sweetly deranged.
The jars had more laughs than any rich treat,
In this honeyed mayhem, our union's complete.

So raise high your spoons, let the sweetness flow,
For every kindred spirit loves a good show.
Beneath the old tree, where our laughter ensued,
We savored the nectar, our spirits renewed.

Citron Conversations

In a citrus grove, we gathered for fun,
With lemons and limes, our friendship begun.
Jokes zested like fruit, tangy and bright,
We laughed with the lemons, a citrus delight.

A lime rolled away, what a cheeky surprise,
As we chased it down 'neath the open skies.
With each silly slip and a citrusy quip,
We bonded through laughter on this fruity trip.

The oranges chimed in, as jokes took flight,
"Who's got the zest for a laugh tonight?"
We peeled back our worries, with smiling faces,
In a citrus assembly, love truly embraces.

So here's to the grove, with all of its cheer,
Where lemons and limes bring friends ever near.
With each witty banter, our hearts intertwine,
In the shade of this grove, it's always divine.

www.ingramcontent.com/pod-product-compliance
Lightning Source LLC
Chambersburg PA
CBHW062111280426
43661CB00086B/448